Kangaroos

ALICE TWINE

PowerKiDS press.

New York

For Julie and Chef Roo
Thanks for all the cinnamon globbobread!

Published in 2008 by The Rosen Publishing Group, Inc.
29 East 21st Street, New York, NY 10010

First Edition

Editor: Amelie von Zumbusch
Book Design: Julio Gil
Photo Researcher: Nicole Pristash

Photo Credits: Cover, p. 1, 5, 7, 9, 11, 19, 24 (top left, top right, bottom right) Shutterstock.com; p. 13 © www.istockphoto.com/Phil Morley; pp. 15, 23, 24 (bottom left) © www.istockphoto.com/Susan Flashman; p. 17 © www.istockphoto.com/Eric Gevaert; p. 21 © www.istockphoto.com/Michelle Gustavson.

Library of Congress Cataloging-in-Publication Data

Twine, Alice.
  Kangaroos / Alice Twine. — 1st ed.
      p. cm. — (Baby animals)
  Includes index.
  ISBN 978-1-4042-4145-9 (library binding)
  1. Kangaroos—Infancy—Juvenile literature. I. Title.
  QL737.M35T95 2008
  599.2'22—dc22
                                                          2007019509

Manufactured in the United States of America

Contents

Do you know what this animal in its mother's **pouch** is? It is a kangaroo! Baby kangaroos are called joeys.

Kangaroos, like this joey, are known for their long legs. Kangaroos can hop as far as 30 feet (9 m) in one jump.

While kangaroos have long legs, they have short **forelimbs**. Kangaroos have **claws** on both their legs and their forelimbs.

9

Kangaroos live in Australia. They live in open woodlands and grasslands.

There are several different kinds of kangaroos. This joey is an eastern grey kangaroo.

13

Red kangaroos live in the dry middle part of Australia. Red kangaroos are the largest kind of kangaroo.

A newborn joey crawls into its mother's pouch. Several months later, the joey looks out of the pouch for the first time.

Joeys drink their mother's milk. Newborn joeys drink only milk, but older joeys eat grass and other plants, too.

Kangaroos often sleep during the day. Young joeys sleep in their mother's pouch. Older joeys sleep on the ground.

A joey and its mother are often part of a bigger group of kangaroos. A group of kangaroos is called a **mob**.

Words to Know

claws

forelimbs

mob

pouch

Index

Web Sites

Due to the changing nature of Internet links, PowerKids Press has developed an online list of Web sites related to the subject of this book. This site is updated regularly. Please use this link to access the list:
www.powerkidslinks.com/baby/kang/